Desert Animals

Armadillos

by Emily Rose Townsend

Consulting Editor: Gail Saunders-Smith, Ph.D.

Consultant: Michael A. Mares, Ph.D.
Director, Sam Noble Oklahoma Museum
of Natural History, University of Oklahoma,
Norman, Oklahoma

Pebble Books

an imprint of Capstone Press
Mankato, Minnesota

Pebble Books are published by Capstone Press
151 Good Counsel Drive, P.O. Box 669, Mankato, Minnesota 56002
http://www.capstone-press.com

1 2 3 4 5 6 08 07 06 05 04 03

Library of Congress Cataloging-in-Publication Data
Townsend, Emily Rose.
  Armadillos / by Emily Rose Townsend.
  p. cm.—(Desert animals)
  Includes bibliographical references (p. 23) and index.
  Contents: Armadillos—Deserts—Body parts—What armadillos do.
  ISBN 0-7368-2075-2 (hardcover)
  ISBN 13: 978-0-7368-9487-6 (softcover pbk.)
  ISBN 10: 0-7368-9487-X (softcover pbk.)
  1. Armadillos—Juvenile literature. [1. Armadillos.] I. Title. II. Series.
QL737 .E23T68 2004
599.3'12—dc21   2002154497

Summary: Simple text and photographs describe armadillos that live in deserts.

Note to Parents and Teachers

The Desert Animals series supports national science standards related to life science. This book describes and illustrates desert armadillos. The photographs support early readers in understanding the text. The repetition of words and phrases helps early readers learn new words. This book also introduces early readers to subject-specific vocabulary words, which are defined in the Glossary section. Early readers may need assistance to read some words and to use the Table of Contents, Glossary, Read More, Internet Sites, and Index/Word List sections of the book.

Table of Contents

Armadillos

Armadillos are mammals.
Most armadillos live alone.

Some armadillos are small. Others are big.

deserts where armadillos live

Deserts

Desert armadillos live in the deserts of Argentina and northern Chile.

Body Parts

Armadillos have armor.
Small pieces of bone
cover their bodies.

Armadillos have
sharp claws.

What Armadillos Do

Armadillos dig burrows
in the ground with
their sharp claws.

Armadillos eat small plants, worms, and insects. Armadillos get water from their food.

Armadillos do not often fight predators. They can roll into a ball, run away, or hide in burrows.

Most armadillos stay
in burrows during the day.
They come out at night.

Glossary

armor—bones, scales, and skin that some animals have on their bodies for protection; an armadillo's armor is small plates of bone covered with skin.

burrow—a hole or tunnel in the ground made by an animal

desert—an area that is very dry; deserts do not get much rainfall.

mammal—a warm-blooded animal that has a backbone; mammals have hair or fur; female mammals feed milk to their young.

predator—an animal that hunts other animals for food; foxes, jaguars, and bush dogs are predators of armadillos.

Read More

Butterfield, Moira. *Animals in Hot Places.* Looking At. Austin, Texas: Raintree Steck-Vaughn, 1999.

Jango-Cohen, Judith. *Digging Armadillos.* Pull Ahead Books. Minneapolis: Lerner Publications, 1999.

Squire, Ann O. *Anteaters, Sloths, and Armadillos.* Animals in Order. Franklin Watts, 1999.

Internet Sites

Do you want to find out more about armadillos? Let FactHound, our fact-finding hound dog, do the research for you.

Here's how:

1) Visit *http://www.facthound.com*

2) Type in the **Book ID** number: **0736820752**

3) Click on **FETCH IT**.

FactHound will fetch Internet sites picked by our editors just for you!

Index/Word List

Word Count: 93
Early-Intervention Level: 13

Editorial Credits
Mari C. Schuh, editor; Patrick D. Dentinger, designer; Kelly Garvin, photo researcher; Karen Risch, product planning editor

Photo Credits
Bruce Coleman Inc./Jeff Foott, cover, 1, 14; George Schaller, 6, 18; Francisco Erize, 10; Jen & Des Bartlett, 12
Corbis/Hubert Stadler, 16
Michael A. Mares, 8
Minden Pictures/Claus Meyer, 20
Tom Boyden, 4